My First Book about the Alphabet of Farm Animals

Amazing Animal Books
Children's Picture Books
By Molly Davidson
Mendon Cottage Books

JD-Biz Publishing

Download Free Books!
http://MendonCottageBooks.com

Read More Amazing Animal Books

Purchase at Amazon.com

Download Free Books!
http://MendonCottageBooks.com

Introduction

Farms are places where animals are kept and used by people.

Seventeen percent of all work in the United States is on farms.

A is for an Anserini, which is the scientific name for Geese.

Farmers raise geese for their eggs.

Their wings are about 1 1/2 times the size of their body; and are very powerful, so if a goose gets annoyed they can seriously hurt a human by flapping their wings.

 **is for Beef Cattle.**

There are many different types of beef cattle, but they are all raised for the purpose of eating.

Cattle live in large herds, where they spend most of their day eating hay, grass, and alfalfa.

There are about 1 1/2 million cows in the World being raised by farmers.

B is also for a Border Collie.

Border collies are bred as herding dogs, and are used to help farmers gather their livestock.

They shed their heavy coat of hair twice per year, once in the summer and again in the fall.

They live for about 13 years.

C is for Chickens.

Humans have raised chickens for their eggs, meat, and feathers for over 10,000 years.

There are more chickens in the World than any other bird.

Chickens are not very good at flying, the longest recorded flight was only 13 seconds.

D is for Ducks.

Ducks are raised for their tasty eggs, and they help eat garden pests like grubs and snails.

The beak of a duck is extra strong, because it is made out of bone.

Duck feathers, called down, are also used in bedding and pillows.

E is for an Equus Africanus Asihus, the scientific name for a Donkey.

Donkeys have been used for over 5,000 years to pull and carry heavy loads.

They usually share a pasture with horses, they help keep them calm.

F

is for a Felis Catus, the scientific name for a Cat.

One of the greatest reasons for a farm to have a cat is for mouse and rodent control.

They have sharp claws with they use to run and to climb with.

G is for a Goat.

Goats are related to sheep, and used for their hair, skin, milk, and meat.

They are also used to help carry heavy loads.

Goats have rectangular shaped eyes, helping them see almost all the way around, without moving their heads.

G is also for a Gayal.

Gayal is a type of cattle found in India and Bangladesh, raised for meat.

In some places, the groom must give the bride's family at least one Gayal in order to marry their daughter.

H is for Horses.

Horses are used by humans all over the World, for transportation, sports, and in battle.

They live for about 30 years, and some can run up to 40 mph.

H
is also for Holsteins.

Holsteins are a milk cow, which produce about 7 gallons of milk per day.

The average person eats about 584 pounds of dairy produces per year, thanks to milk cows.

There are about 350 squirts per gallon of milk.

K

 is for a Kid, which is a baby goat.

A kid takes about 5 months to be born.

They eat have their own call and smell, this is how their mother recognizes them.

Kids are able to walk within a few minutes of being born.

L is for Ladybugs.

Ladybugs are very important for farmers, because they eat aphids and other tiny bugs that like to destroy crops.

They lay about 2,000 eggs per year, which hatch within a few days of laying.

L is also for Llamas.

Llamas are cousins of the camel, and are used for their meat, wool, skin, and to carry heavy loads.

They like to eat grass, plants, flowers, and also need to drink lots of water.

M is for Meleagris, the scientific name for a turkey.

Turkeys have been raised for their meat for hundreds of years.

An adult turkey has over 3,500 feathers.

Turkey is one of the top meats eaten for celebrations like Thanksgiving and Christmas.

 **is for an Owl.**

Barn owls hunt mice and rodents mostly at night, and when they fly they are almost completely silent.

O is also for an Ostrich.

Ostrich farms can be found in more than 50 countries.

They are raised for their meat and to use their skin as leather for clothes and accessories.

They are cheap to raise because they eat less than sheep, pigs, and cattle.

P is for Pigs.

Pork (the meat of a pig) is the most eaten of all meat around the World.

Baby pigs have 28 teeth that fall out when they turn one, and then they grow 44 stronger adult teeth.

 **is for a Quail.**

Quail are raised on a farm like chickens, usually in a pen where they can lay their eggs.

They have smaller eggs than a chicken; they are also used for their meat.

They start laying daily eggs when they are only 6 - 7 weeks old.

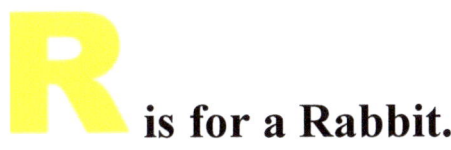 **is for a Rabbit.**

Rabbits are a wonderful farm animal, because they will eat the left over greens from your kitchen and garden.

They are used for meat, which many elderly people prefer to eat above other meats.

R is also for a Rooster.

Roosters are adult boy chickens, which have been found on farms for more than 5,000 years.

They are like an alarm clock and will crow as soon as the sun comes up, letting the farmer know it is time to get up and go to work.

S is for Sheep.

Sheep were one of the first animals to be raised on farms by humans.

They use them for meat and wool; one pound of wool makes 10 miles of yarn!

They eat all types of greens, more than most animals, so they are good at cleaning up what other livestock have left behind.

T is for Trout.

Trout and fish farms are becoming very popular, because many people love to eat fish.

They are raised in big tanks and fed lots of protein and vitamins, which help keep them healthy, and makes their meat healthier for humans.

V

V **is for Vicugna Pacos, the scientific name for an Alpaca.**

Alpacas are raised for their thick, warm hair, called fleece.

They are very kind and gentle animals, that like to live in herds with other alpacas.

 **is for the Western Honey Bee.**

The Western Honey Bee is found on farms all over North America, and they are used for honey production.

A hive can have as many as 40,000 bees living in it at one time.

 **is the last letter in an Ox.**

Oxen have been used to plow fields and pull wagons for thousands of years.

Up to 10 oxen can be yoked together for extra heavy, hard work.

They only sleep about 4 hours per day.

Y is for a Yak.

Yaks are large, hairy, and strong relatives of cattle.

They are used to carry heavy loads and pull farming equipment.

They can weigh up to 2,200 pounds.

Z is for a Zebu.

Zebus are small cattle that can mostly be found on farms in South America, Asia, and Africa.

Since they are a small size they are easier to handle than regular cattle, but are still strong enough to pull loads and farming equipment.

Conclusion

I hope you have enjoyed learning about many different farm animals.

One more fact: on average every farmer provides food for 155 people, in 1960 it was only 25 people.

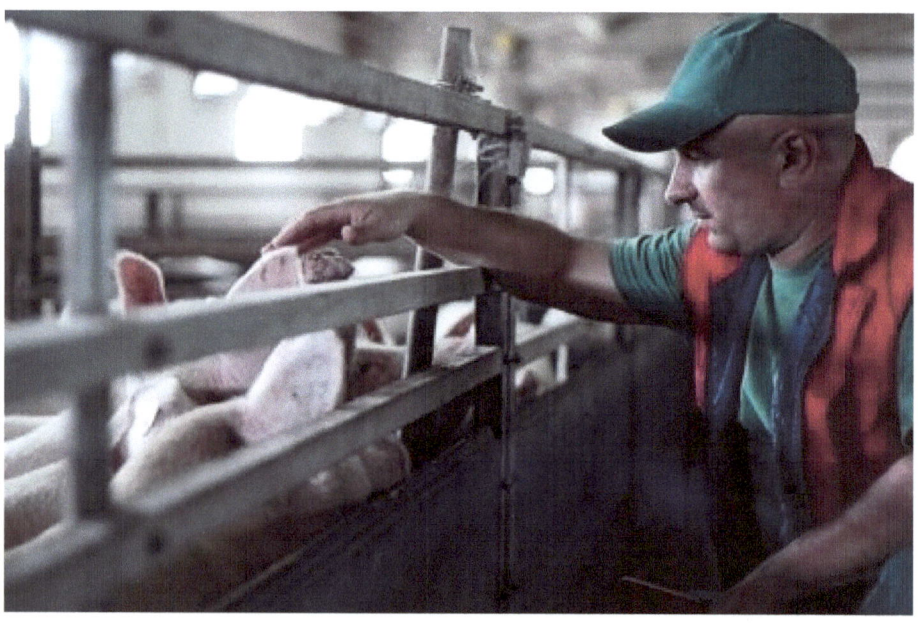

Download Free Books!

http://MendonCottageBooks.com

Horses For Kids
Amazing Animal Books For Young Readers
By John and Annalee Davidson

Ponies For Kids
AmazingAnimalBooks For Young Readers
Rachel Smith

Ten Amazing Horses For Kids
Nature Books for Kids
JD-Biz Publishing
K. Bennett

Akhal-Teke "The Golden Horse of the desert" For Kids
Nature Books for Kids
JD-Biz Publishing
K. Bennett

Suffolk Punch "The Gentle Giant" For Kids
Nature Books for Kids
JD-Biz Publishing
K. Bennett

Shires "The great Horse" For Kids
Nature Books for Kids
JD-Biz Publishing
K. Bennett

Colonial Spanish "Horse of the Americas" For Kids
Nature Books for Kids
JD-Biz Publishing
K. Bennett

Canadian "The Little Iron Horse" For Kids
Nature Books for Kids
JD-Biz Publishing
K. Bennett

Cleveland Bays "History and Future" Horses For Kids
Nature Books for Kids
JD-Biz Publishing
K. Bennett

Our books are available at

1. Amazon.com

2. Barnes and Noble

3. Itunes

4. Kobo

5. Smashwords

6. Google Play Books

Download Free Books!
http://MendonCottageBooks.com

Publisher

JD-Biz Corp

P O Box 374

Mendon, Utah 84325

http://www.jd-biz.com/

www.ingramcontent.com/pod-product-compliance
Lightning Source LLC
Chambersburg PA
CBHW050857290526
45792CB00002B/626